T0196237

Finding the Spirit Within

Finding the Spirit Within

A Self-Guided Mental Health Activity Workbook

Randy Hamelin and Erica McKenzie

Illustrations
Karen Tremblay Kilbride

FINDING THE SPIRIT WITHIN
A SELF-GUIDED MENTAL HEALTH ACTIVITY WORKBOOK

iUniverse books may be ordered through booksellers or by contacting:

iUniverse
1663 Liberty Drive
Bloomington, IN 47403
www.iuniverse.com
1-800-Authors (1-800-288-4677)

ISBN: 978-1-4917-7929-3 (sc)
ISBN: 978-1-4917-7931-6 (e)

Print information available on the last page.

iUniverse rev. date: 11/06/2015

Contents

Introduction vii

Facing Your Fears 1
Moving toward Independence 2
Setting Goals 3
Go for the Goal 5
It's Time to Set Some Goals! 6
Setting SMART Goals 7
Life's Little Obstacles 8
Five Factors That Can Increase Vulnerability 9
Changes 10
All Good Things 11
Focus on the Positive and Eliminate the Negative 12
On the Bright Side of Positivity 13
Face Your Fears 14
Increasing Positive Self-Talk 17
I Am Amazing! 18
Making Connections 23
Communicating with "I" Statements in Four Easy Steps 24
Now It Is Your Turn to Try 25
Want to Be Heard? Learn to Listen 26
Who Am I? 27
My Free Time 28
Getting to Know Yourself 29
The Interview 30
A Gift to Myself 31
Scheduling Enjoyable Activities 32
The Story of Me 33
The Story of Me 34
Combat Stress with Silly Words and Crazy Ideas 35
Fun and Creative Ways to Relieve Stress 36
My Gratitude Journal 37
Love Is in the Air 38
Coping Skills from A to Z 39
Coping Skills 40
Conclusion 41
Reading List 43

About the Authors 45

Introduction

As a registered professional counselor and mental-health therapist, I have found value in providing my clients with as many resources as I can. Therapy is not a one-size-fits-all process. People go through their own journeys at their own paces and utilize information gathered from these journeys in their own ways. When people are given resources in therapy, they are given opportunities to learn and grow. These resources are tools that they can add to their toolboxes in life. When they recognize they are in situations they have difficulty handling, they will have the tools available for them at all times.

For the past ten years, I have been studying psychology and working with individuals and families on their everyday struggles in awareness, stress relief, and mental-health wellness. I found that it was important for my clients to go home with homework after a therapy session. This allowed them to process and think about what they'd learned about themselves during the sessions. Most of my clients would shine throughout the therapy sessions, but when it came to taking what they had learned in the office and transferring that knowledge to the real world, they sometimes struggled. This is where homework helped bridge the gap.

This book is intended to serve as (1) a tool for therapists and clients to use to help transfer skills from therapy into the real world and (2) a self-help workbook for any adolescent or adult not in therapy. I have been giving these same pages to my clients for the past ten years, and it has made all the difference in the success of their therapy progress.

You will find many mental-health, stress, and anxiety workbooks on the shelves of bookstores. What makes this book stand out from others is that I have written it to be simple and user-friendly. I want to keep the focus on the readers' thoughts in the present moment. This will allow readers to experience the worksheets as they complete them. Readers will notice that there is not a lot of extra reading material between worksheets. This is because the entire book is meant to be experiential in nature.

You will find a list of reading resources at the end of this book if you wish to further your knowledge in the field of awareness, stress relief, and mental-health wellness.

The material in these pages is suitable for adolescents and adults who are going through a variety of challenges in their lives. This workbook will help you begin a new journey, set you on a life plan for success, and provide you with tools that you can fall back on in the future.

You can use this workbook as an individual self-guide to your own mental-health wellness. You do not need a therapist in order to use the tools in this book; however, this book should never replace the benefits of seeking the advice of a trained mental-health professional.

The workbook pages are in an order that I have found useful for my clients. The book will start by helping you recognize your fears and bring to the surface an awareness of your unconscious or other issues you may not have thought of before. It moves forward from awareness to developing techniques that will help you through negative thoughts and issues that cause distress.

As you progress through the book, you will find a variety of techniques that you can apply to combat stress, relieve anxiety, and begin to live life to the fullest. Not all the activities will be easy, but in my experience, when we struggle with something, it is often where we need to focus our energies the most.

This book will also give you tips for how to communicate more effectively with others, explain how you are responsible for your own thoughts, and show that only you have the power to change them.

It is my sincere wish for you to have happiness and find the root of your happiness. I hope the tools in the book will help you on your journey—and that you will pass these tools onto others so that they too can shine.

Forevermore,
Randy

Facing Your Fears

Fear and lack of confidence can prevent people from moving toward full independence. Below is a list of items that may add to that fear. Under each, describe a situation or circumstance that taught you to expect the fear of failure, abandonment, or disappointing others. The first sentence in each section is an example.

Fear of Failure

I feel that if I fail, no one will take me seriously.

_____
_____
_____
_____

Fear of Abandonment

I feel that my friends will no longer want to hang out with me.

_____
_____
_____
_____

Fear of Disappointing Others

I feel that I am going to disappoint my parents because they have done so much for me.

_____
_____
_____
_____

What actions can you take today that will help you overcome your fears and increase your independence? Give yourself a deadline for each action, and stick to it.

Action   Date

tell people my plans and goals   August 31

_____   _____
_____   _____
_____   _____

Moving toward Independence

Depending too much on others can cause you to project responsibility of your own "stuff" onto others. It is important that you are able to make decisions and problem-solve on your own in order to achieve personal independence. Below, brainstorm decisions that you have let others make for you in the past as well as decisions you will make for yourself in the future.

Decisions I Have Let Others Make for Me

what college I had to go to

1. _____
2. _____
3. _____
4. _____
5. _____
6. _____
7. _____
8. _____
9. _____
10. _____

Decisions I Will Make for Myself

what friends I will hang out with

1. _____
2. _____
3. _____
4. _____
5. _____
6. _____
7. _____
8. _____
9. _____
10. _____

What are some positive self-messages ("I am kind to others") you can repeat to remind yourself that you are capable of making decisions and being independent?

Post your reminders throughout your living space so that you will see them throughout your day. You may want to get creative and write your messages on fancy paper or use recipe cards and decorate them with your own unique style.

1. _____
2. _____
3. _____

Setting Goals

We all strive to create goals that we hope to accomplish one day. We often set the bar too high, which makes it difficult for us to reach our goals. We then develop insecurities, shame, and disappointment in ourselves. We begin to feel helpless and useless because nothing ever goes the way we want it to.

When we change our goals to be more realistic or break them down into smaller, more manageable ones, we begin to have feelings of accomplishment and success.

Oftentimes the goals we set are not unrealistic, but the approach we take to accomplish the goal is unrealistic. When I create a goal for myself, I create a multistep processes. I begin by setting an end goal. I then create a list, and it becomes my long-term goal list. Next, I write each goal at the top of a page. I write each goal on a separate sheet of paper. It may seem like a waste of paper, but it will be important as we go along.

With the goal at the top of the paper, I begin to write all the steps that will be required to reach the goal. These smaller steps are my short-term goals. Next to each short-term goal, I write a realistic date of when I think I will complete this step or goal. As I write each goal, I think of the SMART goal process by George T. Doran. "There's a SMART way to write management's goals and objectives" [1] Here is an example of a goal:

Goal: Drink Eight Glasses of Water Each Day

- *Specific.* Drink one glass of water every two hours.
- *Measurable.* Make a checklist to keep track of how much water I drink.
- *Achievable.* Set a timer on my phone that will go off every two hours to remind me to drink a glass of water.
- *Realistic.* I am awake for at least sixteen hours a day; therefore, I will be able to drink a glass of water every two hours.
- *Time oriented.* By setting a specific amount of glasses and not just saying that I will increase the amount of water I drink, I can determine how often I need to drink. I can set my day up for success with alarms and checklists.

Once you have repeated this process, you will have a more realistic plan for obtaining your goals. This will help build your confidence by successfully completing each short-term goal and moving toward your long-term goals.

Having a plan like this will help organize your daily routine and enable you to eliminate those feelings of hopelessness and self-doubt.

The plan for each of your goals can be added right into your agenda or daily planner so that you can create a schedule that will direct you toward your goals. One important factor in creating your goals is making sure your goals are specific. The more specific your goals are, the easier it will be to reach them.

The following pages will help get you in a routine of setting and accomplishing goals.

---

[1]   George T. Doran. "There's a SMART way to write management's goals and objectives" (*Management Review*, AMA FORUM).

Goal Plan Worksheet

Use the chart below to start creating your goal plan.

Long-Term Goals	Date to Be Completed	Short-Term Goals	Date to Be Completed	Possible Obstacles
To start living a healthier lifestyle	One year August 1, 2016	Drink 8 glasses of water a day.	August 15, 2015	Forgetting to drink Time
		Walk for 30 minutes per day.	August 31, 2015	Motivation Time
		Go to a yoga class once a week.	August 31, 2015	Motivation Money

Go for the Goal

Short-term goals are essential for self-esteem and a sense of productivity in our daily lives.
Write some goals below that you wish to incorporate into your life.
It is never too soon or too late to get started.
Make your short-term goals simple and easy to accomplish ("brush my teeth").

Today I will

_____
_____
_____

Today I will

_____
_____
_____

Today I will

_____
_____
_____

It's Time to Set Some Goals!

Achieving your goals is not going to happen overnight. Goals must be predetermined, and a plan has to be put into action so that success can be reached.

In the space provided, set four specific goals that you did not set in the previous pages. For each goal, identify possible challenges or obstacles you may face and how you think you will be able to overcome those challenges.

Goal #1

Possible challenges/obstacles:
Ways to overcome them:

Goal #2

Possible challenges/obstacles:
Ways to overcome them:

Goal #3

Possible challenges/obstacles:
Ways to overcome them:

Goal #4

Possible challenges/obstacles:
Ways to overcome them:

Setting SMART Goals

It is important to create goals for all areas of our lives. In the space provided, create a goal for each of the following areas, and describe the first step that you will take to accomplish that goal. Be as specific as you can. You may need to look back at the "Setting Goals" chapter to remind you about SMART goals.

Home Environment

Goal:
First step(s):

Work Environment

Goal:
First step(s):

Education Environment

Goal:
First step(s):

Social Environment

Goal:
First step(s):

Coping and Dealing

Goal:
First step(s):

Other

Goal:
First step(s):

Life's Little Obstacles

We all have personal barriers that sometimes prevent us from acting in our best interest. Read the words below, and circle the ones that best relate to your life. Add your own barriers in the spaces provided.

abuse	denial	pretending
anger	dishonesty	pride
apathy	excuses	regret
avoidance	grief	rigidity
being perfect	guilt	stubbornness
blaming	low self-esteem	vulnerability
confusion	pain	worry

Personal Reflections

_____ is/are my biggest barrier(s).

They/it prevent(s) me from _____.

I can confront this/these barrier(s) by

_____

_____

_____.

Five Factors That Can Increase Vulnerability

There are times in our lives when we are more likely to feel bad about ourselves—or the people around us. We know when we are going through these times when we have low self-esteem, are constantly thinking negative thoughts, isolate ourselves, do not feel supported by others, or do not handle stress the way we usually do.

In the following space, identify ways you can improve these factors so that you can prepare yourself if these vulnerabilities interfere with your progress of reaching happiness.

Which ones are factors in your life? Explain how you can improve these factors.

Low Self-Esteem

Make a list of all the things that I am good at. When I feel sad about myself, I can pick one and do it.

Constant Negative Thinking

Write twice as many positive thoughts in my journal as negative thoughts.

Inability to Express Yourself

Sing out loud, and dance like nobody is watching.

No Social Support Network

Phone Courtney or another friend.

Poor Stress Management

Put on my headphones and go for a thirty-minute walk.

 **Changes**

Change is unavoidable and can cause increased amounts of stress, frustration, confusion, and uncertainty about the future. We all have to change so that we can learn and grow as individuals. To make change easier, answer the following questions. This way, you can better prepare yourself for your new exciting life journey.

1. List circumstances in your life that are contributing to your dissatisfaction, stress, or frustration. Explain why.

_____
_____
_____

2. What circumstances do you wish were present in your life that would increase your sense of personal fulfillment? List them below.

_____
_____
_____

3. What activities do you wish you were more regularly involved in?

_____
_____
_____

4. What changes could you make to ensure you have more time for activities that increase positivity in your life?

_____
_____
_____

5. What, if any, responsibilities would you like to share with others in order to reduce your stress level?

_____
_____
_____

6. Who in your life would you share your responsibilities with to lessen your load? Think about people you interact with every day—family, friends, church members, coworkers, and so forth. What would you like them to do to help you make changes in your life?

_____
_____
_____

All Good Things

To start on the path of positive thinking, answer the following questions. The answers will give you a better understanding of all the positive things around you—and show you what you can do to keep a positive outlook.

List five things that are already positive in your life.

1. _____
2. _____
3. _____
4. _____
5. _____

List five personal strengths that you use to enrich your life and the lives of those around you.

1. _____
2. _____
3. _____
4. _____
5. _____

What simple changes could you make to help bring balance to your life?

1. _____
2. _____
3. _____
4. _____
5. _____

How can you use your personal strengths to bring more positivity and satisfaction into your life?

1. _____
2. _____
3. _____
4. _____
5. _____

Focus on the Positive and Eliminate the Negative

Look at the world around you. Where is there good? Happiness? Contentment?

Using the space below, write a letter to yourself that expresses your happiness, contentment, admiration, or satisfaction with the things you find most important in your life.

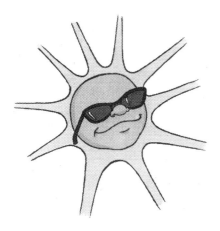

On the Bright Side of Positivity

To help you stay focused on the positive aspects of your life, make a list of the things that you like about yourself, things you like in general, people you like, and things that make you happy.

What I Like about Myself

Things I Like

People I Like

Things That Make Me Happy

Face Your Fears

Negative thoughts and fearful thoughts block self-esteem by holding people back from doing things they enjoy.

Circle the fearful thoughts you most commonly have:

being criticized	others getting mad at me
being left out or behind	others hurting my feelings
failing at something	others seeing me as unattractive
getting fired	others seeing me in a panic
making a mistake	others thinking I'm bad
money	saying/doing something wrong
not being liked	sickness

Now ask yourself what is the worst that could happen if one of the fearful thoughts from the above list actually happened. Be honest.

_____
_____
_____
_____
_____
_____

List below some coping techniques you could use to help yourself work through your fearful thoughts and reduce stress. Add to the examples provided.

Do a reality check with self or others.
Replace fearful thought with a positive, realistic thought.
Use relaxation techniques to help reduce tension.
Affirm your ability to cope using positive self-talk.
Distract yourself with an enjoyable activity.

_____
_____
_____
_____
_____
_____

As a way of maintaining your self-esteem, it is important to keep in mind certain important positive thoughts.

Circle the affirmations below that mean the most to you to help you remember to focus on the positives.

I expect good things.	I like myself.
I am a good person.	Mistakes are learning opportunities.
I have good things to offer.	I know I can do it.
I can trust myself.	I am lovable.
I feel good about me.	I can make good decisions.
I value myself.	No one is perfect.
I can say no.	I can affirm others and myself.
I can be a friend to someone.	I can deal with my fears.
I do not have to be perfect.	I can learn how.
I can grow and change.	I can forgive others.
I respect others and myself.	My family loves me.
I am worthy of love and respect.	Others like me.

Come up with three different ways to help you remember the positive daily affirmations circled above (put them on a mirror, display them in a journal, etc.).

_____
_____
_____
_____
_____
_____
_____
_____
_____
_____

With self-talk, we may be able to change our negative thoughts into positive ones. Self-talk is the silent conversation that continually takes place in our heads.

Self-talk can be so powerful that we can talk ourselves into doing things or out of doing things. Negative thoughts can be changed to positive, supportive, uplifting, and goal directed.

Negative Self-Defeating Thoughts

> I can't.
> I shouldn't.
> I am too tired.
> It's too hard.
> I would but …

Positive Supportive Thoughts

> I am capable.
> I will.
> I know I'll feel better.
> I'll give it a try.
> Why not?

My negative thought _____

Change to positive thought _____

Increasing Positive Self-Talk

It is easy for us to fall into the trap of thinking negative thoughts about ourselves. To help combat those negative self-doubting thoughts that you say to yourself, answer the following questions. Visit this page whenever negative thoughts interfere with your day.

It is important to practice these positive affirmations. Complete the following activity so that your positive self-talk becomes part of your daily routine. It takes twenty-one days to start a new habit. Give it time, and you will start thinking more positive thoughts—even on days you feel things are not going your way.

List five positive views you have of yourself ("I am a great person to talk to," "I am lucky to have had so many successes in my life," etc.).

_____
_____
_____
_____
_____

List five positive views you have of the world ("People enjoy being helpful," "There is empathy out there," etc.).

_____
_____
_____
_____
_____

List five positive views you have of the future ("The happier I am, the brighter my future will be").

_____
_____
_____
_____
_____

Every day, select one of the positive views you listed above and recite it in front of a mirror. Then write it down and post it in a prominent place so that you can refer to it often. After doing this exercise for one week, how has your mood changed?

_____
_____
_____
_____

I Am Amazing!

Do not be so quick to find your faults; you have amazing qualities too! When we are feeling down about ourselves, we assume people are thinking the worst of us. From the list below, circle the words that best describe some of your most wonderful qualities:

accepting	happy	patient
approachable	hardworking	polite
articulate	helpful	practical
attractive	honest	punctual
communicative	humble	reasonable
complimentary	inclusive	reliable
considerate	independent	respectful
creative	insightful	responsible
decision maker	intelligent	sensitive
dependable	kind	sociable
easygoing	leader	spiritual
energetic	loving	talented
enthusiastic	loyal	thoughtful
ethical	moral	trustworthy
faithful	musical	warm
friendly	nonjudgmental	wise
funny	open	
good listener	organized	

Write three more qualities below that are not on the list.

_____

_____

_____

Give the following sheets to three different people who you trust and hold dear. These can be close friends, relatives, or coworkers. Have them fill out the forms and circle the wonderful qualities they see in you.

Dear _____,

You are a person whom I have come to trust and appreciate. Because of this, I am asking for your help in reminding me of what makes me who I am—specifically my best qualities. Please circle the words below that you feel best describe me:

accepting	happy	patient
approachable	hardworking	polite
articulate	helpful	practical
attractive	honest	punctual
communicative	humble	reasonable
complimentary	inclusive	reliable
considerate	independent	respectful
creative	insightful	responsible
decision maker	intelligent	sensitive
dependable	kind	sociable
easygoing	leader	spiritual
energetic	loving	talented
enthusiastic	loyal	thoughtful
ethical	moral	trustworthy
faithful	musical	warm
friendly	nonjudgmental	wise
funny	open	
good listener	organized	

Write three more qualities below that are not on the list.

_____

_____

_____

Thank you so much!
Signed,

_____

Dear _____,

You are a person whom I have come to trust and appreciate. Because of this, I am asking for your help in reminding me of what makes me who I am—specifically my best qualities. Please circle the words below that you feel best describe me:

accepting	happy	patient
approachable	hardworking	polite
articulate	helpful	practical
attractive	honest	punctual
communicative	humble	reasonable
complimentary	inclusive	reliable
considerate	independent	respectful
creative	insightful	responsible
decision maker	intelligent	sensitive
dependable	kind	sociable
easygoing	leader	spiritual
energetic	loving	talented
enthusiastic	loyal	thoughtful
ethical	moral	trustworthy
faithful	musical	warm
friendly	nonjudgmental	wise
funny	open	
good listener	organized	

Write three more qualities below that are not on the list.

_____

_____

_____

Thank you so much!
Signed,

_____

Dear _____,

You are a person whom I have come to trust and appreciate. Because of this, I am asking for your help in reminding me of what makes me who I am—specifically my best qualities. Please circle the words below that you feel best describe me:

accepting	happy	patient
approachable	hardworking	polite
articulate	helpful	practical
attractive	honest	punctual
communicative	humble	reasonable
complimentary	inclusive	reliable
considerate	independent	respectful
creative	insightful	responsible
decision maker	intelligent	sensitive
dependable	kind	sociable
easygoing	leader	spiritual
energetic	loving	talented
enthusiastic	loyal	thoughtful
ethical	moral	trustworthy
faithful	musical	warm
friendly	nonjudgmental	wise
funny	open	
good listener	organized	

Write three more qualities below that are not on the list.

_____

_____

_____

Thank you so much!
Signed,

_____

It really is that simple—you are amazing! Using the three sheets your trusted people filled out, list your top ten qualities below:

1.
2.
3.
4.
5.
6.
7.
8.
9.
10.

Post this page in a spot where you will see it every day.

Making Connections

Communicating with others is not always easy. Use this worksheet to identify some of the struggles that you may have regarding communication. When you identify your type of communication style, you can better understand what you need to change and how your communication style influences how others see you.

- What is most difficult for you when communicating or interacting with other people?
- What do you have the most difficulty with when you are in a group situation?
- Are you a better talker or a better listener? Explain why.
- What skills could you develop that would help you deal with social situations?
- How do you usually handle conversations when you do not know what to say?

List three things you can do in your everyday conversations to improve your connections with others.

1.
2.
3.

What has kept you from trying these ideas in your past conversations? With whom in your life would you like to have a good, honest conversation? Why?

Communicating with "I" Statements in Four Easy Steps

"I" statements are a tool that you can use to better express how you are feeling and why you are feeling a certain way about a certain situation. These statements can be used in everyday conversation and during times of conflict. "I feel good when Sally takes care of me because I feel loved."

Step 1: I Feel

Make an honest statement about how you are feeling in the moment.

- "I feel very angry right now."

Step 2: Because

Use the word *because* to explain why the person's action(s) or behavior(s) is/are triggering your feeling(s).

- "Because you did not pick me up at the time we agreed upon."

Step 3: I Want or Need

Tell the person specifically what you want or need from him or her if a similar situation happens in the future.

- "I need you to be on time in the future. If your plans change or you are going to be late, I would like you to call me."

Step 4: I Will

This is optional, but it can be a powerful add-on if needed. If the problem persists, tell the person what you are prepared to do if he or she does not alter the behavior as requested.

- "If you continue to be late, I will not go out with you anymore."

Now It Is Your Turn to Try

Practice your "I" statements by turning the following "you" statements into "I" statements.

"You never help me clean up around the house! How lazy can one person be? I never want to see your laundry on the floor again—or else!"

I feel _____ because _____.
I want (or need) _____. (I will _____.)

"I can never tell you anything private because you never keep your mouth shut!"
I feel _____ because _____.
I want (or need) _____. (I will _____.)

"Have you never heard of a thing called quiet? I swear you are the loudest person I have ever met!"
I feel _____ because _____
I want (or need) _____. (I will _____.)

Want to Be Heard? Learn to Listen

Nonverbal language is the key to letting people know you are listening to what they are saying. Here are a few tips for practicing effective listening skills. Under each, provide three examples of how you can show people you are listening.

1. Look interested:
Make eye contact.

2. Listen to what the other person is saying:
Ask questions to clarify.

3. Show that you are supportive:
Be kind and honest with your feedback.

Who Am I?

How do you see yourself? Draw a self-portrait on this page.

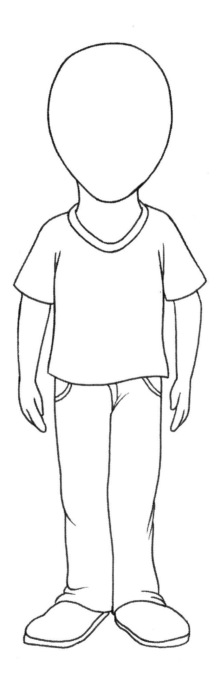

My Free Time

Use this list to brainstorm the things you like to do for yourself:

- adventure activities

- community activities

- creative activities

- cultural activities

- home activities

- outdoor activities

- physical activities

- relaxing activities

- social activities

- solo activities

- spectator activities

- spiritual activities

- volunteer activities

Getting to Know Yourself

Knowing who you are and determining what you want out of life are important steps for becoming a happier, more positive individual. Use this worksheet to reflect on who you are.

If I could travel to any place in the world, I would go to _____.

I am most proud of myself when _____.

My happiest moment was when _____.

If I could change one thing about my life, it would be _____.

My biggest fear is _____.

My unhappiest moment was when _____.

The hardest thing I deal with on a daily basis is _____.

The thing I most look forward to every day is _____.

I feel bad about myself when _____.

It is difficult for me to tell others that _____.

I feel comfortable telling others that _____.

If I could be any part of nature, I would be _____.

If I could be any animal, I would be _____.

The most important thing I want to know about myself is _____.

_____
_____
_____.

The Interview

We can gain insights about ourselves by asking those who know us best. Our perceptions of what we think people know about us are often misjudgments. Use this worksheet to learn a little more about yourself by interviewing someone who has known you for a while.

An Interview with _____

Q: _____?
A: _____.
Q: _____?
A: _____.
Q: _____?
A: _____.
Q: _____?
A: _____.
Q: _____?
A: _____.
Q: _____?
A: _____.
Q: _____?
A: _____.

A Gift to Myself

At this point, you have worked so hard that you deserve a reward for all the effort you have put into completing this book. Use this worksheet to come up with a list of rewards for yourself.

- My most cherished memory:

- My favorite thing to do on a lazy afternoon:

- Foods I like to indulge in:

- Emotions I like to have:

Scheduling Enjoyable Activities

Think about some activities that you find pleasure and relaxation in. What about them is enjoyable for you? What benefits to receive from participating in them? Make a list below.

My Enjoyable Activities

- What I find enjoyable about them:

- The benefits I receive from participating in them:

The Story of Me

We each have our own stories to tell. Using the next two pages, create a story outline about yourself. This will give you an opportunity to reflect on your journey so far, and it will keep you on the right track to success.

My story begins with

_____

_____

The easiest part is about

_____

_____

The hardest part is

_____

_____

The happiest part is

_____

_____

The saddest part is

_____

_____

I would not include

_____

_____

The longest part is

_____

_____

The shortest part is

_____

_____

The Story of Me

Things I can do to feel better about myself:

_____
_____
_____

Activities I enjoy doing:

_____
_____
_____

My proudest moments include:

_____
_____
_____

Goals I have set for myself:

_____
_____
_____

I would describe myself as:

_____
_____
_____
_____
_____

Combat Stress with Silly Words and Crazy Ideas

What do these mean to you? In the space below, write what you think the following sentences mean. Use these stress-relieving strategies when you are feeling overwhelmed and stressed. The first one is done for you.

- Wear rose-colored glasses—and look at the positive side of things.

- So what?

- Dream on.

- The other side of the fence has greener grass.

- Candy should not be taken from babies.

- Lemonade makes life better.

- Rock on.

- Another day begins tomorrow.

- Open mind, open heart.

- Leaping to conclusions is only good for leapfrogs.

- Wisdom of an old horse.

- Doors make poor windows.

- Take a vacation from your island.

- Row, row, row your boat.

- Fantasize reality.

Fun and Creative Ways to Relieve Stress

Add your own ideas in the blank spaces provided. Cut them out, place them in a jar, and pick one when you are feeling stressed.

Ride a horse	Pet a dog	Paint a picture
Watch the clouds roll by	Jump on a trampoline	Play catch
	Go for a swim	
Go to the movies		Listen to music
	Delight in doing nothing	Read in a hammock
Plant flowers		
Write a letter to a loved one	Savor a cup of tea	Take a bath
Explore the woods	Toss a Frisbee	
	Call a friend	Watch a favorite childhood cartoon
Twirl!		Play a board game with friends
	Meditate	
	Eat an ice-cream cone	Use sidewalk chalk
Cuddle with a kitten		Listen to nature

My Gratitude Journal

By looking at the things that you are most grateful for, you are creating a positive inner dialogue with yourself that will help keep you focused on a positive path toward happiness. In the space provided, make a list of the things that make you feel grateful. I give you permission to write the silliest of things. Imagine your life without a toilet—or something else silly.

I encourage you to make this a part of your daily practice and reflection.

I am grateful for:

Love Is in the Air

Use the space below to write a letter to someone who you care for very much. This could be someone who has been with you through good times and bad—or someone you have always had a close connection with.

Tell the person what he or she means to you and how the person has helped you. Be sure to include something you do not tell them often—or perhaps thank the person for something you sometimes take for granted.

Sharing your expressions and thoughts of love and caring with others goes a long way toward doing the same for you.

Coping Skills from A to Z

Add your coping skills beside each letter of the alphabet so that you have a go-to list when you are struggling with negative thoughts, feelings, or behaviors.

A	Accepting
B	Begin reaching out to others
C	Creative expression
D	Deep breathing
E	Emotional awareness
F	Forgiving
G	Goal setting
H	Humor
I	Inner strength
J	Journaling
K	Keeping in touch with friends
L	Leisure time
M	Meditation
N	Nature appreciation
O	One step at a time
P	Patience (with self and others)
Q	Quality "me" time
R	Recreation
S	Sleeping well
T	Time management
U	Understanding myself
V	Volunteering
W	Walking
X	Expressing myself
Y	Yearly checkups
Z	Zestful living

Coping Skills

In the space provided, create a list of coping skills that are related to a specific area in your life that you struggle with. You may use some of the tools you have learned in this book—or you can create your own.

My top coping skills when I am feeling _____:

1.

2.

3.

4.

5.

6.

7.

8.

9.

10.

Conclusion

As we navigate through our lives, we sometimes have ups and downs. When we are given the tools to help get through the down times, we flourish and maintain positive streams of happiness. I hope that this workbook has given you tools to help you get through the tough times—and that you will return to this workbook whenever a challenge presents itself in your life.

One of the biggest gifts you can share is giving your love and support to someone else. If you have learned something from this book, pass it along to someone who could use some help.

This book is not a substitute for a mental-health professional. It is always a good idea to seek the advice of someone who has formal training and can provide you with additional resources and advice.

Not all therapists are the same. You may have to visit more than one before you connect with someone who understands you. You can use this workbook as part of your therapeutic journey—or you can use it before you start therapy to identify the areas in your life that need improvement.

In whatever way you choose to use this book, I hope the tools I have provided are helpful. Remember to stop, live in the moment, and enjoy your new path to happiness.

Reading List

I have enjoyed reading and learning from the following books. Please take the time to pick up one of them at your local bookstore or library.

Achor, Shawn. *The Happiness Advantage: The Seven Principles of Positive Psychology That Fuel Success and Performance at Work.*

Cain, Susan. *Quiet: The Power of Introverts in a World That Can't Stop Talking.*

Chodron, Pema. *Taking the Leap: Freeing Ourselves from Old Habits and Fears.*

Chopra, Deepak. *The Ultimate Happiness Prescription: 7 Keys to Joy and Enlightenment.*

Chopra, Deepak. *The Soul Of Leadership: Unlocking Your Potential for Greatness.*

Davidson, Richard J. (with Sharron Begley). *The Emotional Life of Your Brain.*

Dyer, Wayne. *Excuses Begone!: How To Change Lifelong Self-Defeating Thinking Habits.*

Dyer, Wayne. *The Power of Intention.*

Epstein, Mark. *Thoughts without a Thinker.*

Fox, Michael J. *Always Looking Up: The Adventure of an Incurable Optimist.*

Gladwell, Malcolm. *Outliers: The Story of Success.*

Gladwell, Malcolm. *Blink: The Power of Thinking without Thinking.*

Gladwell, Malcolm. *Tipping Point: How Little Things Can Make a Big Difference.*

Goldberg, Natalie. *Writing Down the Bones: Freeing the Writer Within.*

Goldberg, Natalie. *Thunder and Lightning: Cracking Open the Writer's Craft.*

Goldberg, Natalie. *Wild Mind: Living the Writer's Life.*

Goldman, Daniel. *Social Intelligence: The New Science of Human Relationships.*

Gray, John. *Men Are from Mars, Women Are from Venus.*

Katie, Byron. *I Need Your Love: Is That True?*

Siegel, Daniel. *Mindsight: The New Science of Personal Transformation.*

About the Authors

Randy Hamelin is an entrepreneur; a college professor of business, communications, English, and psychology; and a writer who has developed many skills through his career, education, and training.

Additionally, he holds a master's degree in counseling psychology and is a practicing registered professional counselor and psychotherapist. He is an avid equestrian and created an equestrian facility with his family. They train, compete in equestrian events, conduct corporate retreats, and serve organizations and individuals in business, health care, and education.

He lives with his family and herd of horses in southern Ontario, Canada.

New for 2015
Defining Normal: A Guide to Living a Happy Life.
Defining Abnormal: What Not to Do if You Want a Happy Life.
Finding the Spirit Within (Daily Journal)
www.randyhamelin.com

Erica McKenzie is a certified child and youth counselor and professional life coach working privately and out of Country Sunset Stables near Windsor, Ontario, Canada.

Erica has worked with children and youth since 1994 as a youth programmer and supervisor for the City of Windsor's Parks and Recreation Department and as a residence-life coordinator at the University of Windsor.

She holds two degrees in education, including a master's degree in education. Erica is a member in good standing of the Ontario College of Teachers and the Ontario Association of Child and Youth Counselors. She is certified with Equine Assisted Growth and Learning Association (EAGALA).

She is a volunteer and board member at the Windsor Youth Centre, a safe space for homeless and at-risk youth.

Her passion is her love for animals—the most important is Dora (seen above)—and she utilizes her talents as the team leader for the Windsor Chapter of Therapeutic Paws of Canada, a volunteer-based, animal-assisted therapy program.

A proud introvert, Erica is currently researching techniques for helping introverts embrace their quiet ways while maintaining positive balance in their sometimes "noisy" lives.

https://recreatingsimplicity.wordpress.com

Printed in the United States
By Bookmasters